AGING With GRACE

Published by Willow Creek Press
P.O. Box 147, Minocqua, Wisconsin 54548

For information on other Willow Creek Press titles,
call 1-800-850-9453

Printed in The United States of America

AGING *With* GRACE
{Whoever She Is}

By **MARY MCHUGH**

⊞ WILLOW CREEK PRESS®

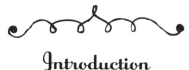

Introduction

This book is for women who find their fifties closing in on them. It's an attempt to prepare you for the signs of aging before they catch you by surprise. Little things, like a noticeable stomach that used to be flat. Or not being able to remember the name of that nice woman across the street. Or only being able to text with your reading glasses on. It will answer crucial questions like: Why is everyone talking so fast on television? How did the Rolling Stones get to be so old? Who knew Keith Richards could write a book? Where did those lines around my mouth come from all of a sudden?

So I thought I'd help all of you baby boomers out there slide through your fifties, sail through your sixties, triumph over your seventies, and enjoy your eighties. Somehow I woke up one day and found myself 80 years old. I have no idea how that happened, but I seem to be having the time of my life anyway. My life is full of surprises and possibilities. This is my 21st book. I'm tap dancing on YouTube. My husband and I go out on a date every Friday. My grandchildren are still talking to me. And I ride on a merry-go-round every Tuesday. According to a recent study, the peak of happiness comes at age 85. My life is full, rich, abundant with possibilities and I want yours to be too.

There are certain tricks that will get you through the whole aging thing with as few glitches as possible. The main thing is to keep your sense of humor and roll with the punches.

Part 1

Sliding Through Your Fifties

This can be your best decade so far. I know, I know. You're old enough to join AARP. Men don't follow you down the street just to look at you—although you look pretty damn good for 50—or any age for that matter. The truth is: your children are almost raised and on their own; you and your husband can take a weekend or a week off and just enjoy each other. If you're not married, you can relax and enjoy single life or go on eharmony and see what's out there. In other words, you're freer, more confident, better looking, more competent and just a dynamite woman. Go for it!

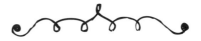

How to fight off the urge to email your old boyfriend.

It's not that you don't love your husband. He's funny and smart and a great father and he remembers your birthdays and anniversaries. He tells you he loves you and you know he does. It's not that you want to sleep with somebody else.

It's just that your old boyfriend still thinks of you as young and exciting and spontaneous and hasn't lived with you for the last 25 years. He doesn't know that you hate to clean, are bored with cooking every night for the last 25 years, that you think football is just big hulks crashing into one another, that you sometimes play spider solitaire for hours when you should be ironing or doing wash or shopping for kitchen curtains.

He thinks of you as that girl who was ready to go anywhere, do anything, dance the night away, say things that make him laugh, tell him he's gorgeous and perfect and you'll love him forever.

Well, you're not that girl any more. No one is that girl anymore after 25 years of marriage and three children, a job, a house and responsibilities. You're a full-grown woman, an adult, a responsible human being—most of the time.

It's just that every once in a while you get an email from him asking if you're still married and how you are and if you're happy. He shouldn't be doing that, of course, because he's married and has children and is not supposed to be thinking about an old girlfriend.

You know he's not going to leave his wife and run off with you to Hawaii even if you said you were ready to go with him for a forbidden lei.

But how could one innocent email hurt? Just a "Hi. How are you? What's new in your life?" Just a friendly hello to—what? To remind him that you're still around? That you're still that interesting woman he fell in love with? Face it—you're a tease.

Here's what you do instead:

Plan a weekend alone with your husband
at an inn somewhere you both love.

Make him a Julia Child recipe and
serve it to him by candlelight with
flowers and you dressed in silk.

Go on a sunset sail with him.

Send him a long email telling him
how much you love him and how
glad you are that you married him.

Rent a Pink Panther movie and
watch it in bed with him because
laughter is the best aphrodisiac.

Pick one night a week for a date night
with your husband and don't let anything
get in the way of keeping that date.

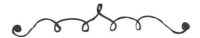

How to get your teenager into college and how to pay for it without losing your home.

First recognize the fact that there's no way to save enough money to put three children through college and maybe graduate school and have any money left for retirement. When you and your husband are 65 (or whatever age retirement is by then) you're just going to have to move in with whichever child has a job and is supporting himself until his children are ready for college, in which case, I assume you'll be dead and it's his problem.

Here are some ways to scrape up $40,000 for his freshman year in college. (I'm only using "he, his, him" because it's a drag writing "he/she, his/her, him/her every time I refer to your child. Please don't write to me if you are the head of NOW.)

1. Get a job(if you don't already have one, and if you do, hang on to it and get a huge raise). First, lower your expectations. If you were the vice president of a corporation before you had children, it's hard to convince a Human Resources person that you are the perfect person for this position.

Actually, you're way over-qualified for this position. For the last 16 years or so, you have been organizing the lives of four people (especially your husband), supervising the scheduling of a complicated household, negotiating peace among three completely different entities (your children), keeping within a budget, staying calm while all about you there is chaos, ending the year with a profit that you wisely invested in what you mistakenly considered the children's "college fund." Unlike certain other large organizations, the government did not bail you out when the market crashed taking your college fund with it. They just taxed you more.

So you need to get a job that makes sure you're home by 3 when your teens are home. Otherwise, as I don't have to tell you, they'll become drug addicts, alcoholics, pregnant at 14, or join the Tea Party. What kind of jobs are there that pay at least $40,000 a year, allow you to be home by 3:00 and leave you with enough energy to cook dinner every night and help your husband find his socks?

Well, you could write a best-selling book, but statistics show that most writers make about $5,000 a year, and unless you are famous or infamous, no publisher will even talk to you, unless you find a brilliant, far-sighted publisher like the one who is bringing you this book. And it's even harder finding an agent who is willing to take on an unknown writer than it is a publisher. First, you have to be a best seller and then a flint-hearted agent will gladly take 15% of your earnings and sell your next book. Back to the drawing board.

How about starting your own business? Sounds good, right? You set your own hours. You're always available when your children or your husband needs you. You could open a boutique with just the right kind of clothes that all your friends are looking for but can't find in department stores or other shops. Great idea. But you'd probably use up that $40,000 just getting started and you won't earn it back, to say nothing of the $40,000 you need for your college-aged child, for years. And what if you guess wrong about your friends? What if they've decided to go a whole different way than when you first thought of this store?

Or you could teach. Sounds good until you look into what teachers do. You think, Oh, I'll be working the same hours the children are in school. I'll have summers off. I'll be with children all day and I love children. But actually, you have to go back to school to get certified to be a teacher, since schools wisely frown on good-hearted people who "just love children" and think they can teach. You have to spend your time after school before you fix dinner grading papers while settling arguments among your children, pacifying the child who is mad at you for taking a job, and persuading your husband that you can do all this without ruffling a feather, messing up your hair, or losing your sex drive entirely.

I think we've come to a sales job. When I was growing up a long, long time ago, my mother's idea of the most dreadful end for any woman was to end up a saleslady at Lord and Taylor because she didn't save her money or marry a rich man. Nowadays, if you go to most department stores, you will search long and hard to find even one saleslady per floor. Do you need help finding a size or a decent dress to wear job hunting? It's a desert out there. Harder to find a salesperson than a drink of water.

Maybe a supermarket clerk? Home by 3. No complicated problems to work out. When you're through each day, you're through. No papers to grade, no inventory to check, no employees to pacify. Just check out people's groceries and go home. First you have to get rid of that little voice in the back of your head that says, "You went through four years of college and two years getting a masters in political science to be a supermarket clerk?" You probably aren't too good for this job, but you'll resent having to do it every day.

So what's left? A scholarship? I've heard of college scholarships for students who are very good water polo players, or volleyball champions, or soccer players. I've heard of brilliant students who have a perfect grade point average, an unheard of SAT, who were heads of the student council, editor of the newspaper, built houses in Mexico during their spring vacation, donated a kidney to a poor child in Africa, who couldn't get scholarships because their parents had the bad luck to earn a substantial salary each year. So if your child is under 6 foot 4 and wasn't a great basketball player, or weighed under 300 pounds and couldn't bash people as a football player, he's out of luck for a scholarship.

You might as well face it. You'll have to use your retirement fund to send your child to college, or borrow money from one of those bailed-out banks or forget sending your kid to college.

2. Send him down to the basement to invent a new use for the internet. Encourage him to become a billionaire.

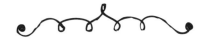

What to do when there are no more children at home.

For 25 years you've been programming three children, each one totally different from the others, to grow up to be successful, happy, contributing, confident, independent people and now all of a sudden—where did those years go? The youngest is off to college and you've got the whole house to yourself. Except when your husband comes home, he's at the peak of his career in his mid-fifties and works harder, travels more, and is distracted more when he is home.

You're on your own, and you're torn between guilty pleasure in long days with nothing you really have to do unless you want to, and guilt that you don't feel useful anymore. You have this uneasy feeling that you should be doing something, but nothing really appeals to you.

You could get a job. Check above to
see if you really want to do that.

You could volunteer at the hospital or
at a nursery school or at your church,
synagogue or mosque.

You could sit by the fire and read all
the books you've always wanted to
read but never had time for.

You could go to graduate school and
get a masters in social work and
become a therapist.

You could lose 20 pounds.

You could take advantage of your
new freedom and look for new
adventures to spice up your life.

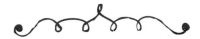

What to do when your college graduate moves back in.

One of my friends suggested that before your college graduate thinks of moving back in, you should change the number on the front of your house. "He will probably be texting and drive right on by," she said. But that seems a little drastic.

After all, you're talking about a child you love. You missed him when he was away at college, and now you have the chance to cook his favorite food for him and do his laundry and make his bed all over again and... uh-oh. What's wrong with this picture?

I don't really have to spell it out for you—right? Your whole purpose when you were raising him was to make him independent, able to support himself, live on his own, marry some nice girl, have children and make you a grandmother. So if you encourage him to settle in and let you take care of him again, you're doing what they call in those 12-step programs "enabling."

Why should he venture out into that cold, cold world to find a job that he doesn't really like, that doesn't pay enough for a decent apartment, and doesn't leave him any money for fun after his monthly college loan repayment? Because that's what he's supposed to do. If you keep taking care of him, why should he leave?

I know. What if he's hungry or cold or sad or can't go skiing with his friends? What if it makes you happy to have him home again? Someone to talk to, someone to run errands for you when you're busy with something else. Someone who has always been the joy of your life. Are you thinking of his best interest—or yours?

Here's my own six-step program (I can't think of 12 steps) to get him to leave:

If you're working, leave the house early and come home after dinner.

Play reruns of "Golden Girls" whenever possible.

Take pictures of him when he's at his most unattractive and post them on Facebook.

Encourage your husband to tell long boring stories about looking for a job when he was your son's age.

Wash his underwear with your husband's madras sport shirt so they come out lavender.

Adopt another child.

Or you can bring in the big guns.

His older sister—to ask questions that
will drive him out of the house:

Are you
still here?

You're getting an
allowance???!!!!

How old are
you anyway?

You're not letting Mom do
your laundry, are you?

You're getting
fat.

Did you call all the
people I told you
to call for a job?

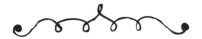

What to do when all your friends are babbling about their grandchildren and your children aren't even married yet.

First, don't blame your friends. They can't help it. Grandchildren are absolutely one of life's great blessings. I have three and I know. The best part is you're not at all nervous when you're taking care of them because you've done it all before. You know they won't break. When they smile at you, when they recognize you when you come to babysit, when they first say, "Nana", or "Nanny" or "Gramma" or "Nonny" or whatever they feel like calling you, you know the heavens have smiled on you.

That said, you've got to figure out a way not to hit your friends when they talk about all the miraculous things their grandchildren have done that week.

Here are a few suggestions:

Ask, "Has your daughter
married the baby's father yet?"

Tell your friend to bring her grandchild
to lunch the next time so you get a
chance to hold a baby again.

Change the subject.

Here are some other things to talk about:

Betty White and Sarah Palin

Dancing With the Stars—Who Are These People?

Does any airline still give you free food?

Do you think Jeb will come
out of the Bushes and run?

Are you going to get an electric car?

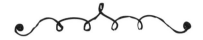

How to lose 20 pounds before your next high school reunion.

You're not really fat. Your clothes are just a bit tight in the middle. But you want to look not just good but smashing. You want to make all those boys sorry they didn't marry you. So you've got six months to lose those 20 pounds. How do you do that? Here are all the ways I've lost 20 pounds over the years. They all work, but somehow those 20 pounds keep creeping back on and I have to do it all over again. But don't look beyond the high school reunion. Concentrate on being svelte for that one glorious night.

My chocolate and wine diet: No I didn't just stuff my face with Godiva chocolates and drink wine all day long. But I knew that I would never stick to any diet without a hit of chocolate every day and a glass of wine with dinner.

So I found some delicious cookies made by Bahlsen called Afrika cookies that are only 20 calories each and I keep them downstairs in the basement refrigerator so I won't eat the whole box at once. I'm lazy so I only have a couple during the day. And even Jane

Brody of the *New York Times* says chocolate is good for you: "Chocolate is replete with substances that may actually enhance well-being as well as improve one's mind. It can stimulate the mind and may delay some of the ravages of advancing age." And Jane Brody should know. She writes a health column every week for the *Times* and she's as thin as their newspaper on Mondays. Anyway I cut down on the calories, do some boring exercises and grab a cookie every once in a while and sip a Chardonnay with dinner. And it works. I lose the 20 pounds—and of course put it right back on.

Or you could try the South Beach Diet. My husband's doctor suggested he try the South Beach Diet because it's healthy and cuts down on belly fat. "Let's try it," I said, not realizing that I would be cooking and chopping and shopping and slicing and dicing for the next few months as we lost the belly fat, as promised and had a great time doing it because we were spending more time together, talking and tasting and laughing and getting thinner. This diet does work but you have to really like cooking.

My favorite way to lose weight is on Jenny Craig's food. Over the years I've gone to Jenny's diet centers and with the help of their skilled and really nice counselors, I've always lost the weight I wanted to lose, but once I leave their centers and their wise advice, I put the weight back on. Right now

I'm back on Jenny Craig because they have a new, really good feature, which is home delivery. You give them your credit card number and they send you two weeks or four weeks supply of delicious food and snacks and a counselor calls you from California or wherever she lives and helps you through the times when you're tempted to add 1000 calories at a wedding or dinner party. And she nudges you into being more active than just walking your dog every day. They have pancakes and brownies and cheesecake and pizza and chicken fajitas and yummy things that actually make you lose weight. I don't know how it works, but it does.

I lost the most weight when my appendix burst and I spent two weeks in the hospital eating hospital food. 20 pounds lost just like that—but I really don't recommend this way of losing weight.

Unless you change all your eating habits and exercise habits you'll keep putting the weight back on. But it's worth losing that 20 pounds for your high school reunion. "You look fabulous!" they'll say. And you will.

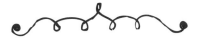

How to get through menopause without turning into a bitch.

Lots of luck with this one! I thought I breezed through menopause because I really didn't have all those hot flashes—except in the middle of the night—so I didn't start fanning myself in public or turn bright red and sweat on a freezing January day. And I avoided most of the 35 (35!) symptoms of menopause listed by the Association of Women for the Advancement of Research and Education (AWARE):

Symptoms of Menopause

Hot flashes, flushes, night sweats and/or cold flashes

Irregular heartbeat

Irritability

Mood swings, sudden tears

Trouble sleeping (with or without night sweats)

Irregular periods; shorter, lighter periods; heavier periods, flooding; phantom periods, shorter cycles, longer cycles

Loss of libido

Dry vagina

Crashing fatigue

Anxiety, feeling ill at ease

Feelings of dread, apprehension, doom

Difficulty concentrating, disorientation, mental confusion

Disturbing memory lapses

Incontinence, especially upon sneezing, laughing

Itchy, crawly skin

Aching, sore joints, muscles and tendons

Increased tension in muscles

Breast tenderness

Headache change: increase or decrease

Gastrointestinal distress, indigestion, flatulence, gas pain

Sudden bouts of bloat

Depression

Exacerbation of existing conditions

Increase in allergies

Weight gain

Hair loss or thinning, head, pubic, or whole body; increase in facial hair

Dizziness, light-headedness, episodes of loss of balance

Changes in body odor

Electric shock sensation under the skin and in the head

Tingling in the extremities

Gum problems, increased bleeding

Burning tongue, burning roof of mouth, bad taste in mouth, change in breath odor

Osteoporosis (after several years)

Changes in fingernails: softer, crack or break easier

Tinnitus: ringing in ears, bells, 'whooshing,' buzzing, etc.

Good grief! I'm certainly glad I didn't know about all these symptoms while I was going through menopause. And I'm really sorry I know about them now. Now that I've seen this list, I think I had a lot of irritability—but it seemed justified at the time. I was working as an editor at a weekly magazine and certain people kept irritating me. (Was it just me?) And I did have "disturbing memory lapses" but I just thought it was because I wasn't 20 anymore. And I did gain weight, but see above for how I got rid of the extra pounds—again—and again—and again.

I certainly would have noticed "electric shock sensation under the skin and in the head"! or "tingling in the extremities" or "tinnitus."

What I realized years later was that I definitely had my bitchy moments, but it was like I had waited my whole life to answer back. (I called one man in my office a "little prick". He didn't mind the "prick" part as much as the "little".) I'd always been such a good girl. Always pleasant and nice and smiling and co-operative. Sometimes I felt like my smile was frozen on my face because I was trying so hard to be agreeable. So I kind of enjoyed being a bitch, but I don't get much chance to be one anymore. Nobody likes an old bitch.

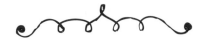

How to explain why your 80-year-old mother is tap dancing on YouTube.

You could accept your husband's explanation that senility is settling in and you can expect more bizarre behavior from your mother (he always thought she was bizarre anyway.) But you know you're really lucky to have a mother who tap dances on YouTube or anywhere else.

Engrave in your mind your conversations with your friends who have mothers the same age. Think of your friend who has lost her mother to Alzheimer's. Her mother doesn't know her when she visits her in the nursing home. Think of the friend whose mother calls her every day to tell her all the things she's doing wrong. At least your mother is too busy dancing to worry about your behavior. Or the friend whose mother drinks all day long because she doesn't have anything else to do. Your mother may drink a little but at least it leads to dance.

Dancing seems like the least worst thing she could be doing. Of course, we have the question, "Why is she doing it on You-

Tube where all your friends can see her?" In other words, why doesn't she just do it in the privacy of her own home and make a fool of herself alone? I asked several women in their 80's why they think women of a certain age—certain age!! More like way beyond certain—would go on YouTube at all.

Here's what they told me:

Because Tap Dancing Granny
got more than 50,000 hits.

Because people all over the world
comment on what great legs they
have—not all of them perverts.

Because it's more fun than playing bridge.

Because their friends say "You're amazing!"
(even if they really mean "You've lost it!")

Because W.H. Auden said: "Dance till
the stars come down with the rafters.
Dance, dance, dance till you drop."

Part 2

Sailing Through Your Sixties

60 used to be old. But that was in the days when women didn't have much to do after they raised their children or retired from their jobs. They just babysat their grandchildren, cleaned the house, volunteered at the hospital or meddled. I think it's all the exercise and the interesting work we do and the healthy food we eat that make us look much younger than we are. And we've learned so much along the way that people actually ask for our advice. Savor it!

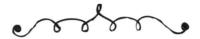

Will you still need him, will you still feed him when he's 64?

When he gets older losing his hair,
Many years from now.
Will you still be sending him a valentine
Birthday greetings bottle of wine.

Sure you will! He may be an old baldie or a comb-over, but you remember him when he had so much hair you used to reach up and smooth it back—like Barbra Streisand did with Robert Redford in "The Way We Were." Sighhhh. He'll always be your valentine and you're happy to share that bottle of wine on his birthday.

If he'd been out till quarter to three
Would you lock the door,
Will you still need him, will you still feed him,
When he's sixty-four.

As if he could stay awake until quarter to three! Dream on. And you'll always need him and you'll always feed him. Although dinner out once in a while would be nice.

> *You'll be older too,*
> *And if you say the word,*
> *He could stay with you.*

He'll always be a year older than you. And you still have all your hair and thanks to your hairdresser it will never be gray. Face it— you'll say the word. He can stay. Where else is he going at 64?

> *He could be handy, mending a fuse*
> *When your lights have gone.*
> *You can knit a sweater by the fireside*
> *Sunday mornings go for a ride.*

Fat chance. You're way past knitting a sweater by the fireside. You just organized a fund-raiser for breast cancer research and you're getting your master's in public administration so you can run for office. It's ok if he wants to mend a fuse, though. And he can go for that ride on Sunday mornings by himself. You need to sleep in.

Doing the garden, digging the weeds,
Who could ask for more.
Will you still need him, will you still feed him,
When he's sixty-four.

You can ask for a lot more than doing the garden and forget digging those weeds. Encourage him to dig those weeds any time he wants though. You need him for that and for picking up stuff at the store when you're busy and how about letting him feed you when he's sixty-four.

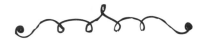

How to sort out ipads from iphones from ipods from blackberries from whatever they think of next.

Last Christmas I wanted to get one or all of those things but I didn't know which ones I really needed, which ones I could afford to add to my phone bill, which ones would bring me into the 21st century where I am fumbling along with a cell phone I almost never turn on and which doesn't even take pictures.

Then I had lunch with a really smart friend of mine in her sixties who has a magic iPhone that does amazing things. But the most incredible thing it did was to receive a film of her first grandchild being born in the delivery room. Her son filmed Olivia being weighed minutes after she was born and then he sent the priceless little movie to my friend outside in the waiting room. Is that the best thing you've ever heard of!

She gets up-to-the minute films of her granddaughter smiling and moving and stretching and it's as if she's right there.

The iPhone of course, does all kinds of miraculous things. It has an app for every occasion from reading the *New York Times* to finding a Valentine's present for your husband. I was going to get that immediately but then I found out it would add a lot of money to my monthly phone bill. An ipad is really neat but it's too big to carry around and I don't care if I don't get my email immediately when I'm out doing other stuff. And an ipod would be good if I wanted to listen to music while walking around. But I don't.

So where does that leave me? I just settled for a phone that would take pictures of anything interesting happening around me—in case George Clooney should sit across from me on the subway or Charlie Sheen should invite me up to his hotel room.

Questions to ask yourself if you are trying to decide which one of these things to buy:

Don't I waste enough time playing spider solitaire on my computer at home without playing it on the train?

When did a book or a newspaper get too heavy to carry on the train?

What's next after texting—smoke signals?

What makes me think my teenage grandchildren will actually text me if I add all that money to my phone bill?

What's the next evolutionary stage for mankind—no personal contact whatsoever—just grunts and nods?

What if the mother of that cute little girl I just took a picture of has me arrested?

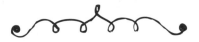

How to feel like you matter when you're the mother of the groom at the wedding.

Your son has found the perfect girl. She's sweet and kind and adores your son and pretends that she thinks you're wonderful. Her parents are nice people and are paying for the whole huge expensive wedding and you don't have to do a thing but pay for the rehearsal dinner.

Here's some tips for mother-of-the-groom behavior:

Don't say to the bride's mother at the rehearsal dinner, "My son was a mess last night! I was afraid he wasn't going to go through with the wedding."

Don't look better than the bride's mother at the wedding. She and her husband are paying for it. Wear a dress that makes you look a little fat. You can look gorgeous at your daughter's wedding.

Take the bride out to lunch before the wedding and tell her how happy you are that she's marrying your son and how much you love her.

Don't ask the bride how soon she plans to start a family.

Don't threaten to kill yourself if the bride decides to keep her own name.

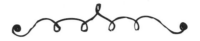

How to stay sane when your husband retires.

Remember how you used to say, "Some day we'll be able to do all the things we always wanted to do. Some day—after you retire—we'll travel all over the world. We'll just be together and have fun." Remember that? What you forgot was that he would be home—all day, every day, all the time, morning, noon and night, every minute. You forgot that you got used to total freedom to go where you want, do what you want, do nothing if you feel like it. Now, he's always wandering into the kitchen or your work room and saying things like, "What's for dinner?" or "Have you seen the remote for the TV?" or "Where do you keep the oregano?"

Here are some coping mechanisms to keep you from running away from home:

Train for a marathon. You have to be out of the house running several hours a day. Or better still, get him to train for a marathon.

Persuade him to volunteer at the hospital or reading for the blind or helping at an old age home three or four or five days a week.

Teach him to blog. He'll never leave the basement.

Leave books on meditation retreats all over the house. Pack his bag for him when he decides to go on one.

Or—you could just enjoy having him all to yourself again and cherish the conversations and sweet lovemaking all over again.

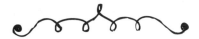

How to adjust when you sell your house and move into a condo.

Rule Number 1: Start throwing things out at least ten years in advance.

I know. You love your house. Your children grew up there. There's room to store everything you've ever owned. There are beds for any child or grandchild who comes to visit. Your garden is finally the way you want it to be with azaleas and daffodils in the spring and roses in the summer and herbs just outside the back door for easy picking.

But look out the window. The leaves from the oak trees are starting to fall. The lawn will soon be covered with them and guess who will have to get out there and rake them? Your husband will be watching football, your sons are in college or in their own apartments without a thought in the world that their aging mother is out there raking leaves and cursing and swearing.

And in another couple of months the first snowstorm will make the driveway undriveable and the path to the door unwalkable.

That boy down the street will grudgingly shovel them for about $50 if he can take time off from his texting.

So slowly, inevitably, sadly, you realize that a condo is the best solution to encroaching unwillingness to deal with all those seasonal nuisances. You find a realtor who shows you a condo with almost enough space and a clause in the deed that says the owner of the condo is responsible for everything outside your door—the roof, the lawn, the driveway, the walks, the trees—everything.

Now we get back to that throwing out part. This is the hard part, until you start doing it and realize how much junk you've accumulated over the years. So start with the place where you put everything "because you might need it some day." The attic or the basement or the room over the garage. Just go in there with a box of large green plastic bags and label on "Get Rid of", one "Give to Some Unsuspecting Friend", and one "Take With Me and Keep until My Daughter Has to Throw it Away When I Die."

Let me give you a little help here since I've done this several times:

Divide these up into whichever bag they belong in:

Books you've read, will never read, you've had since college, or reference books published in 1954.

All old suitcases without wheels.

Anything from the 70's.

45 records you have no way to play—especially Randy Newman's "Short People Got No Reason to Live."

That dollhouse furniture you were going to give to some hospital—do it!

The sewing machine you haven't used in 20 years.

The clothes you keep thinking you'll fit into again—you won't.

Remember when 60 was old?

Well, it isn't anymore. Here's a partial list of women
who are so beautiful nobody believes they're over 60.

Meryl Streep—61   Susan Sarandon—63   Goldie Hawn—64   Jessica Lange—61

Raquel Welch—69   Olivia Newton John—61   Diane Sawyer—64   Diane Keaton—64

Julie Christie—69   Blythe Danner—67   Arianna Huffingrton—60   Catherine Deneuve—66

Part 3

Triumphing Over Your Seventies

Well, I have to say your seventies are a little tricky. That's when the rest of the world tries to make you irrelevant. You're not going to an office anymore, your children introduce you to their friends as "my mother" instead of by your name, people listen to you with eyes glazed over because they are sure ahead of time you can't have anything very interesting to say, strangers start calling you "little lady" or "ma'am", and each birthday starts with a 7. Well, screw 'em! Get out there and dance, meet new people, try new things, go new places. You've got lots of time left. Use it!

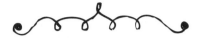

How to communicate with your teenaged grandchildren.

I'm not sure I can help you here. I've tried everything. The main problem is that I don't text. Mostly because I don't want to add a large sum to my phone bill every month. Most people these days seem to accept that as a fact of life. Bigger phone bills.

But it's not just that. It's that you can't really say all the things you want to say texting. If I want to tell my grandchildren that I think they're wonderful, that I love them, that I miss them, that I have a new book coming out, that I'm hosting an online tv show, that I need to know what to give them for Christmas, I need room to say all that. They're too busy to be bothered with emails. They haven't got time to sit in front of the computer and Skype me. So I've tried to figure out how to reduce my questions to texts (if I decide to add all that money to my phone bill, that is). Here's what I've come up with and I'm open to suggestion:

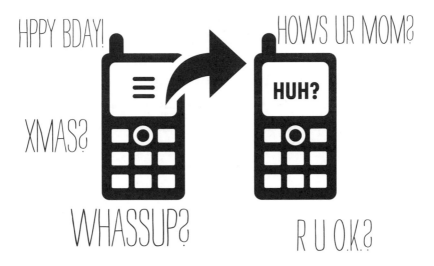

It's no use. I can't do it. I want words brought back. I want the world to go back to talking to each other. I want my grandchildren to call me up and tell me all the things that are happening in their world. What they're doing with their friends. What college they want to go to. What kind of music they are listening to. What movie did they just see. What interests them in this world with 24-hour news coverage.

And what happens to this wordless generation when they grow up? Will they just blink twice for yes and once for no? Will they propose to the person they want to marry by rubbing noses? Will teachers be replaced by remote controls?

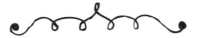

How to convince people you can still walk and talk at the same time when you're in your seventies.

The best thing that ever happened was when they passed some law that said employers couldn't ask the age of a person applying for a job. As George Burns said, "Young. Old. Just words." And he lived that way right up until the day he died at 100. They are just words.

It's one of the last prejudices allowed. You may be 70 and look 50 and as long as the person you're talking to doesn't know you're 70, he or she talks to you as if you're relevant, intelligent, a member of the world that counts. But just slip once and mention that you actually saw Frank Sinatra at the Paramount when you were a teenager or that you remember Pearl Harbor because your father was drafted, or that you know how to jitterbug. The very fact that you even know the word jitterbug plunges you into old ladyhood.

Something happens behind the eyes of the person you're talking to who is in her forties or fities. Uh-oh. Old Person Alert. And she starts talking a little slower and a little louder. She assumes you don't have a computer or a cell phone or an iphone. She says things like, "Oh you don't look a day over 65," or "Do you have any pictures of your grandchildren?"

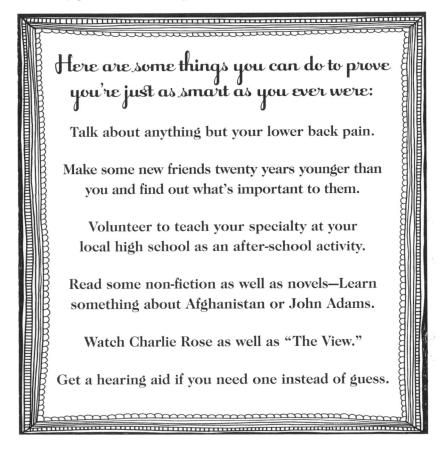

Here are some things you can do to prove you're just as smart as you ever were:

Talk about anything but your lower back pain.

Make some new friends twenty years younger than you and find out what's important to them.

Volunteer to teach your specialty at your local high school as an after-school activity.

Read some non-fiction as well as novels—Learn something about Afghanistan or John Adams.

Watch Charlie Rose as well as "The View."

Get a hearing aid if you need one instead of guess.

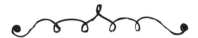

How to understand all those TV shows with disgusting housewives being mean to each other and somebody named Snooki letting her breasts hang out.

I thought maybe I'd get some clue about all these reality shows with people being mean to each other when Snooki, the star of "Jersey Shore" went on David Letterman. I love David Letterman so I thought he wouldn't have anyone on who wasn't at least interesting.

And I was right. She was interesting—in the same way a horrible accident is interesting. First of all she's short. I mean short. If she were an inch shorter she would be a legitimate member of the little people. But she was wearing 6 inch heels so she was almost the size of a regular person. And her boobs threatened to burst through her dress every time she took a breath.

What will this person talk about, I wondered. Well, it seems she had started off the day with a drink. "A shot", I think she said. Because she had been up until four the night before and so it seemed natural when she woke up to go to a bar and have a drink to get her day going. Some people drink coffee. And she talked about being arrested for making some kind of disturbance on the beach. "It was the beach!" she said as if we should all understand that. But the police didn't understand that and handcuffed her and took her off to jail. Just another fun day for Snooki.

I have a feeling I'm not fulfilling my promise to help you understand Snooki and the other reality shows. Let me try with the "Real Housewives of New Jersey." It seems when they are all sitting around the table having dinner and get into an argument, the normal thing to do is stand up and overturn the table onto the person you're having an argument with. Well, isn't that the way you solve arguments in your house? No? Thank goodness. I thought I was past it.

Oh and it seems another way to get your own show is to have six or eight children and have cameras following them around wherever they go and it helps if you and your husband hate each other and get into fierce fights whenever possible. That doesn't appeal to you either? I feel better.

I tried to think of a reality show I could have here in our house but I'm afraid the cameraman and director would fall asleep before they filmed even one episode. I don't think there's much of a market for a show called "We're Still Alive."

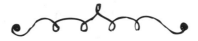

How to get a hearing aid without feeling like your grandmother.

The first thing you need to do is notice the hearing aids your friends are wearing. Actually, you can't notice them because they're practically invisible. The hearing aid is either behind their ears hidden by their hair with the thinnest of cords connecting to the part that fits inside their ears. And some of them don't even have cords. Just a tiny, tiny little thing that fits inside the ear. So forget about the kind your mother had that was clearly visible across the street. Nobody will ever know you're wearing one unless you tell them.

The only difficult part seems to be when you're in a room with lots of people talking and making noise. Like a restaurant or a party. Then it seems to be hard to hear the person you're talking to. But console yourself with the fact that even people with perfect hearing have trouble in a noisy room.

The minor inconvenience of hearing aids is worth it to keep from having conversations like this:

YOU:
"Good morning honey. What would you like for breakfast? How about a fried egg?"

HIM:
"Who died?"

YOU:
"Nobody died. Fried."

HIM:
"Somebody died on Friday?"

YOU:
"NOBODY DIED! I'M HAVING SCRAMBLED."

HIM: "What a terrible way to die."

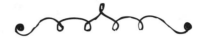

How to accept the fact that global warming is real and you have to take your own bags to the grocery store.

When I go to my daughter's house, there are bags full of every kind of paper—bags, newspapers, milk cartons—bags full of bottles, glass and plastic, bags full of soda cans, soup cans, tomato cans. They're all going some place to be recycled, but the truck that takes them away only comes twice a week, so there's all this stuff everywhere. I know they're saving the environment and I should be too, but it's all I can do to take the newspapers and wine bottles to the dumpster every day.

I asked my three grandsons to give me reasons why I should fill my house with trash, and since they've been taught since kindergarten that we have an obligation to save our planet, they gave me some really good reasons. Here they are:

1. To reduce global warming

Carbon dioxide is a major contributor to global warming and manufacturing certain products releases a lot more carbon dioxide than recycling them would. Making new aluminum products produces 95% more carbon dioxide than recycling old objects.

And for every ton of paper that is recycled, 15 trees are saved. And trees absorb almost 250 pounds of carbon dioxide a year.

2. To prevent air pollution

Factories that manufacture things made from plastic and metals release large amounts of toxic gases. As the population grows, more goods are manufactured filling the air with more toxic gases. If we don't recycle, we have to open more factories with more gases.

3. Scarcity of Landfills

We're running out of places to put our garbage. This is especially bad in cities and suburbs where landfills are creeping closer to people's homes. This makes us vulnerable to diseases.

4. To prevent water pollution.

Waste in landfills seeps into the groundwater and pollutes it. Also scarcity of landfills forces us to dump waste into oceans. This has a devastating effect on marine life.

5. To save energy

Recycling uses much less energy than making them new. Recycling paper saves almost 65% energy than making new sheets of paper. If one pound of steel is recycled it saves ehough energy to light a 60 watt bulb for 24 hours.

Just writing this all down has convinced me. Maybe I can find some really nice-looking boxes to throw everything into.

8 Ways to Get through February

Sleep with someone who thinks you're perfect.

Buy something soft, blue and velvet.

Watch an old Peter Sellers movie—
"Pink Panther" or "A Shot in the Dark".

Think of Jon Stewart's face when he said,
"Thank you Jesus," after Sarah Palin
said she could see Russia from her house.

Have lunch with a person who makes
you feel good just to be alive.

Find a child and go for a sleighride.

Write a blog even if no one reads it.

Start drinking an hour earlier.

Part 4

Enjoying Your Eighties

I have to say, I'm still getting used to that 8 in front of my age. It's really hard to believe that 80-something isn't old. But I'm discovering a lot of it is really in your attitude. I always believe you should try something new to stir up your brain and get you dancing again when you feel yourself in a rut.

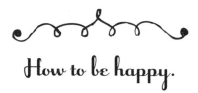

How to be happy.

Do you know they just did a bunch of studies proving the older you are the happier you are? That happiness peaks at 85! And I don't mean senility-happy when you can't remember all the things there are to be unhappy about. I mean real happiness. It seems the time when you're the least happy is when you're 46. Well, duh. That's the time when you have teenagers living in your house. The same children who were delightful and funny and worshipped you are now aliens who find everything you do either disgusting, ridiculous or hopelessly out of date. So it's no wonder that's not exactly the happiest time of your life.

But as those same children grow up, leave the house (well a lot of them do), marry and have children who again find you perfect before they lapse into teenhood, you just get happier and happier.

A lot of it is you have lived such a long time your priorities are in order. If you've lived through the death of a child or a broken marriage or the loss of your parents and the sagging of your face, you know there's very little to be really upset about. Somehow you live through anything life throws your way. You get through to the other side and life goes on. You're still here. There's nothing for it but to make the most of every minute you have left and think of it all as an adventure.

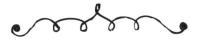

How to think of life as an adventure.

Remember back there in the chapter about what to do when there are no more children at home? And remember that list of adventures I suggested you try. Well, your eighties are the best time to follow the yellow brick road and embark on a whole bunch of adventures.

Every day is an adventure if you make it one. It doesn't have to be floating over the meadows and fields in a hot air balloon or snorkeling in Belize. It can just be walking to a pond nearby and sitting under a willow tree with a book. It can be making a baby laugh when you kiss her toes. Or watching a kitten play with a ball of yarn. Something new, something a little different, something to get up for. A way to get out of your chair in front of your computer and move. Walk, swim, dance. Move.

You may want to try some of my adventures or you might want to find some of your own. The idea is to stretch your mind a little, find something beautiful you've never seen before, have lunch with someone you haven't seen in a while but who used to be a good friend. Think of the things you love to do and find a way to do them, learn something new, reach out, try something different, carpe diem.

In other words—surprise yourself a little every day. Wait until you try it—you'll be amazed at the brain cells you stir up, the ideas you spawn, the fun you'll have.

So take my hand and come along with me to my version of *Alice in Wonderland*. Discover this glorious life, this rich and abundant adventure just waiting for you when you look for it.

So—follow the rainbow:

Take a tap dancing class.

I have a tough time getting myself to exercise in the wintertime.
But there is one kind of exercise that I love—tap dancing. I think
I learned to love tap dancing when I was six years old at the
same time Shirley Temple was six years old and dancing in the
movies.

So I signed up for a class at the Y and every Saturday I put on
my red tap shoes that I've had since college and join nine other
women, all ages, and a lone man to learn a routine which we
will perform at the end of our ten classes. An hour of flap-ball-
changes and shuffle-hop-steps and I am in heaven.

Find an island.

I think it's the idea of an island that I love. A place in the middle of a river or a lake or the ocean, sitting there all by itself, with its own quirky personality and new people, new scenery, new experiences.

Once I went to Governor's Island in New York. It was a warm day so I stopped to sit on a bench in the shade and enjoy the view of the river and the ocean liners docked nearby. I was feeling peaceful and glad I had come, when all of a sudden, out of nowhere, the sound of a woman singing—like the Lorelei—rose up out of the water. "Where are you going? Where are you going? Can you take me with you?" she sang. "Wherever you go, I'm by your side and wherever I go you're with me."

I couldn't believe it. Where was it coming from?

I walked over to the railing by the river but could see no source for this beautiful music coming from nowhere and stood still until it stopped as suddenly as it had started. All I wanted to do was go with her, whoever she was, to hear that lovely voice forever.

Later on I googled the island and found out that my moment of magic was provided by an artist named Susan Philipz singing "By My Side" from the 1971 musical "Godspell." There were speakers somewhere on Lima Pier directed toward the Statue of Liberty. "I have chosen to sing a devotional song, a song of love and adoration that addresses the statue directly," the artist said. It was such a magical moment hearing music coming from the water asking me where I was going when I wasn't expecting it.

Visit a winery.

There are 6,223 wineries in the United States. (As of 2010.) Most of them are in California (3,047) but there are a lot in Washington, Oregon and New York too. And almost every state has at least one winery. Just go to www.allamericanwineries.com and click on their winery locator to find one near you.

I went to some wineries in Sonoma Valley in California one time and had the best time. It's not just tasting all that delicious wine—although that's a major pleasure of this experience—but most wineries have a really good restaurant and an excellent gift shop. Great Christmas, birthday, anniversary, Valentine's Day, Mother's Day, Father's Day, any old day presents. And the tour guide to the winery usually has wonderful stories about the region, how the winery started, who planted the first grape seed. It's fun and you just feel good while you're there—a little wine doesn't hurt.

Go to a toy store.

There must be at least one child in your life who can give you an excuse to go to a toy store for the sheer joy of it. Or you can volunteer for some organization that buys toys for children who don't have any. But it's so much fun—especially if your children and grandchildren are grown and it's been a long time since you went in a toy store and wanted to buy everything on all the shelves.

There are toys to ride on and things to push. There are toys that make noise and little swings. There are cars to ride in and houses to play in. There are crayons and chalk and books to look at. Everywhere there are imaginative toys by Fisher Price and Little Tikes and Play School. A miniature barbecue grill and plastic hamburgers and hot dogs, and spatulas to go with it. Everywhere there are toys stacked on shelves.

This adventure is meant to revive the child inside you, even in your eighties—maybe especially in your eighties. That long ago lost part of you that played just for the pure joy of playing. The part that didn't have to do anything useful or serious.

Maybe you could buy a box of magic markers and send a picture to a grandchild for a change.

Read *The Artist's Way* by Julia Cameron.

I know, people are always saying "This book changed my life." But this book really did change my life. It teaches you to be creative in every area of your life, primarily with exercises designed to get you thinking in new ways by writing morning pages that clear your brain of all the dross that collects there and points you to what really matters to get you where you want to go, and by sending you on artist's dates where you do something you really want to do, not something you're supposed to do or somebody told you you should do it. This incredible book sharpens your senses, opens you up to all the small and large miracles just waiting to be found, helps you find what really matters to you the most.

Go on a house tour.

I always avoided house tours because I thought they would be boring. Who cares about other people's houses, I thought. But then I went on one and found that it was fascinating to imagine what the people who lived in a house were like. There are clues everywhere—family pictures on the walls, books and magazines on the coffee table, bright colors everywhere or pale neutral colors, unusual bathtubs or four poster beds. And in one house there was one sentence framed on the wall. It said, "I think of you in colors that don't exist." What a perfect way to describe love, I thought.

Make your own YouTube.

I always thought it would be fun to make movies, and last Christmas I got a digital camera which allowed me to make three-minute movies. I read about YouTube and decided to try it. I thought "No one will want to see an old lady's movies, but who cares, I'm going to do it anyway just to see if I can."

So I figured out how to put my camera on the tripod I had saved from my portrait-taking days and put a mirror in back of the camera so that I could see what the camera saw, and I produced, directed and acted in eight three-minute movies.

My first movie was called "The Hat Lady" in which I told the story of my life in hats: the sequined black veiled hat I wore to my gynecologist's one day; the black and red Cat in the Hat hat my grandson got at a bar mitzvah and gave to me; the Elvira wig I wore to an editorial meeting at the bridal magazine where I worked; and the large fur hat with the hammer and sickle insignia on it I bought for my husband in Kiev.

Since then I have produced 28 more movies that have had more than 50,000 hits and I discovered that I could make a much longer movie on my webcam and zap it up to YouTube. There's no stopping me.

You may be thinking, "This woman has way too much time on her hands," or you might be saying, "It's never too late to try anything" and you'll be well on your way to avoiding Little Old Ladyhood.

Give an interesting women's lunch.

I learned this adventure from my younger daughter who lived in Boston. She used to invite women she met and wanted to know better to a restaurant for lunch and made some really good friends that way. Since I live in a house, I invited some women for lunch and it turned into a fascinating exchange of ideas and points of view. There was a playwright, a writer whose book was late made into a Broadway play, a woman who ran a management consultant company, a book agent, an actress who also played the harp.

Discussions ranged from the current political campaign to the latest play on Broadway to a book someone loved to the latest gossip about a movie star to someone else's trip to Alaska. We started talking the minute we sat down for drinks and didn't stop until the last bit of Julia Child's Three Fish Terrine was gone. My frozen lemon dessert got the praise it deserved and coffee in the living room mellowed us into reminiscences of unforgettable moments in our lives. They left smiling and we had all exchanged business cards and email addresses.

Buy a keyboard.

When I was a little girl, my mother wanted me to play the piano because she had always wanted to play the piano herself. I was about 6 when Miss Gemberling came to our house to give me piano lessons, and the only part I didn't like was the practicing.

Then, my father who had always wanted to play the piano took lessons from Miss Gemberling too, and when he sat down at the piano I wanted to sit next to him. When I was 8, my father and I played a duet from Die Fledermaus at a recital for 8-year-olds. My father loved it. An old lady in the audience said "Young man, you have courage." He was so young and full of life and he loved me.

Finally my mother gave up and realized I would never be a concert pianist and let me stop taking lessons.

When I was about to celebrate my 70th birthday, I had the urge to play a piano again, so my sweet daughter bought me a keyboard and then secretly wrote to everyone I'd ever known and asked them to send her sheet music that would mean something to me with a note on it telling me what I meant to that friend. Lots of people sent me "New York, New York," and "Les Feuilles Mortes."

I have to admit I'm glad my mother made me take piano lessons because that keyboard and all that sheet music with personal notes from my friends brings me enormous pleasure.

Make a few meals that take longer than 17 minutes to cook.

I must say all the thrill of cooking exciting meals has worn off. I think it was about 1981 when I realized that spending one or two hours concocting some taste thrill was no longer fun.

I just considered food something you had to eat to stay alive. As Julia Child said when I interviewed her for *Cosmopolitan* and asked her if her mother was a good cook, "Cooking was not an art form in our house."

Julia's book *Mastering the Art of French Cooking* came out while I was a young mother raising two daughters and trying to cook for my lawyer husband who had been brought up by his grandmother who was a demon cook. She was also a demon, but never mind—that's another story. I was not a demon cook but it was the 60's and I was supposed to please my husband.

Then along came Julia Child and "The French Chef" on public television and I bought all her books and tried.

I made her crepes for Sunday breakfast, burned myself badly dropping chicken Kiev into hot oil, made a paella declared a triumph by my husband, mastered the boeuf bourguignon which

I still make on an occasional Wednesday when I want to make my retired husband smile.

This was also the time of Craig Claiborne and Pierre Franey who produced great recipes in the *New York Times* every week and I still have their yellowed, precious recipes in my book of classic recipes from my days of gourmet cookery.

For the last few years I've been at home writing books and magazine articles, and by the time the dinner rolls inexorably around every night, I try to put a little effort into something different, something delicious for my ever-hopeful husband, but they're usually tried and true recipes that I've been making for years. My husband likes them but frankly I'm sick of them.

So when I'm in a good mood, I go to www.epicurious.com and conjure up some lovely taste treats that take more than 17 minutes.

Feng shui your house.

For a while there, everyone was feng shuing their houses. I bought a book by Terah Kathryn Collins called *The Western Guide to Feng Shui*, which told me how to do it so that I would be prosperous, happy, fulfilled, and in perfect harmony with the universe. Worth a try, I thought. I started out with the room I work in, sleep in, think in, my favorite room in the house.

Terah told me to divide the room into six sections: one for romance, one for riches, one for family, one for spirituality, one for career, one for fame. I started out with romance because that's my favorite thing and hung a large photo by Robert Doisneau called "The Kiss" a picture of a man and woman kissing in Paris in 1950, the year I pretended to study there and was always kissing somebody.

Next I attacked the "riches" section. The author told me to fill this corner with everything that suggested wealth to me, and what I wanted to buy with all the money that would surely come pouring in as soon as this room were feng shuied properly. I put up a large poster of The Arc de Triomphe, over a little model of the house we stayed in on Cape Cod when the children were little, a glass of sand from the Cape, a Limoges light house, and a tin full of foreign money.

In the "family" section I put up a large poster of Renoir's "A Girl With a Watering Can", framed pictures of my daughter and her husband with their three sons, my mother and father, my daughter who died, my brother. And one of my husband and me on our 50th anniversary.

In the "fame"section, Terah told me to put pictures of people I respect and honors I have received. That was easy. I put my husband's picture in the middle, my father who was an MIT graduate who worked in the Office of Research and Development during World War II on radar, my daughter who earned a masters at Harvard after becoming blind, and my other daughter who brought up three perfect sons and is my best friend. For the honors part I had a couple of awards that I won for my book "Special Siblings: Growing up with Someone with a Disability," and I put them next to the photographs.

Spirituality was next. I don't go to church anymore, but I have a deep faith in God or the Universe, or Cosmic force or Spirit that has given me enormous strength to deal with the death of my daughter, growing older, watching my husband grow older.

I hung light blue rosary beads on my mirror that I bought at Notre Dame Cathedral in Paris. I also have the little bear dressed in an angel dress with gold wings and a halo that says "I'm your guardian angel—I'm your special friend" that my daughter bought for me just before she died. There's another little angel that was given to me by Vicky Sheppard, an angel herself, who was my brother's caretaker at the home in Florida where he spent the last 35 years of his life. And finally, I put the gold cross my daughter wore next to the rosary beads on the mirror.

All that was left was the career part to feng shui. The author told me to put whatever accomplishments I had in that section. By that time, I had written about 15 books—seven serious, seven humorous, and I put them on the shelf of my closet.

Maybe my new TV show on www.familynetworktv.com is a result of my feng shuiing. That would take care of career, fame, riches (maybe). Family, spirituality and romance are humming along nicely—I'm a great grandmother, for example.

Anyway, give it a try. At the very least you'll have an adventure. At the very most you'll be rich and famous and happy.

安　平　和

tranquility　peace　harmony

Design your own website.

While I was interviewing teens for my book of advice to teens growing up with a brother or sister with a disability, I talked to one boy whose brother had a bi-polar disorder who was often violent. He told me he often had to lock himself in his room to keep from being injured or killed by his brother and he found a site where you could set up your own web site—for free. He set up a wonderful one for others like himself with a brother or sister with a disability and gave some valuable advice to them about how to survive. I asked him how to do that and he said to go to www.freewebs.com and they would give me a choice of templates for my own website and walk me through the steps to design it. And the best part was it was all free. He was right. I did all that and soon I had my own web site: www.marymchughwriter.webs.com.

This was so much fun, I set up another free web site in which I wrote blogs and posted videos. It's called "Tap Dancing, Labyrinths, Carousels and My Chocolate and Wine Diet" and you can find it at: www.marymchugh.webs.com. I wrote blogs on hospice volunteering, Pro-choice, National Novel Writing Month, "Julie and Julia", Looking for the Magic, and 101 Things to do Before I Die. I still don't know how to get people to read those blogs and comment on them, but maybe this book will help. Anyway, it was an adventure doing them, and I recommend it.

Get a tarot card reading.

I don't like to admit that I'm intrigued by tarot cards but I can't help it. I'm very suggestible—I once had a whole baby under hypnosis—so you can get me to believe anything. A friend of mine reads tarot cards and she once told me I was going to be on Oprah's show. I laughed and said, "Oh Janet, it's every author's dream to be on Oprah, but it just doesn't happen to most of us."

The very next day, I got a call from a producer on "The Oprah Winfrey Show". She was planning Oprah's last season on television and she was responding to an email I sent describing the impact that Oprah's seminar on Eckhart Tolle's book *A New Earth* had on me. I learned to live in the present, this moment, not worrying about past mistakes or future disasters.

I didn't get on the Oprah show, but I still think it was remarkable that Janet told me the day before that I was going to be on there. And who knows? I still have a few years to meet Oprah and tell her how much she has helped me.

If you're a skeptic, you'll say, oh this is all nonsense. The reader just picks up clues from the way you talk and dress and act, and makes up stuff that would be true for anyone. But I think a truly sensitive psychic can tell you things you didn't know you knew.

Record for the blind and dyslexic.

You've probably already discovered the rewards of volunteering if you're my age.

I'm convinced that the best way to help other people is to do something you really love so that you're not doing it out of a sense of duty but because of the satisfaction that comes with it.

Two years ago I came across an article I had cut out of a magazine about recording for the blind and dyslexic. Because I truly love to read and because my daughter was blind, I called up the RFB&D (Reading for the Blind and Dyslexic and now called Learning Ally because it includes everybody) in New York (my favorite place) and volunteered.

My day in New York reading everything from James Agee's *Let Us Now Praise Famous Men*, to books on psychological conditioning to Simone de Beauvoir's *The Mandarins* has become my favorite day of the week. I've met fascinating people who love books and reading as much as I do.

I had thought I was helping the blind and dyslexic! Actually, I was helping myself spend a perfect two hours.

Meditate in a bubble bath.

Meditation always sounds like a great idea. You just sit there
and concentrate on your breathing, letting the world go by,
allowing thoughts to intrude and float out of your mind, finding peace and happiness. But I found it wasn't so easy. My mind
was a whirlwind of thoughts and worries and things-to-do and
memories. It wouldn't sit still long enough for me to achieve that
peace and happiness

Then I discovered that filling up the and bathtub to the top with
bubbles and sinking down into the warm soapy water was the
best way to relax and for a few minutes I turn off my thoughts
and let the quiet take over. I find myself smiling, and my body
seems to float in the warmth of that tub. I feel renewed.

I don't know if I'll ever be good enough at meditation that I can
carry that peaceful feeling into my real life when I step out of
the bathtub. The world is too much with me, as Shakespeare
would say. But I do think a little of that quiet peace remains and
helps me to let go of the things that don't really matter. Anyway,
it's worth a try. Think of it as another adventure.

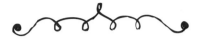

And here's the happy ending.

Whether you're in your fifties, sixties, seventies, eighties, or even nineties or 100 (centenarians are the largest-growing part of the population), you can face it all with grace and style and your own particular brand of courage.

If you think of your life as a tapestry, you'll be grateful for the bright yellows and sweet pinks and pale blues that represent love and joy. You'll recognize the neutral background as the daily sameness that makes up so much of our lives. You'll remember the dark blues, blacks and browns as the troubles we all must face at some time in our lives and know that they give the tapestry strength and that they make the beautiful reds and greens and turquoises that showed you got through them somehow, stand out even more. The thread of bright red running through the whole embroidery of life is the thread of hope that's always there, if you'll let it be.

I do hope I meet Grace one of these days. Like the song says:

"Through many dangers, toils and snares
I have already come;
'Tis Grace that brought me safe thus far
and Grace will lead me home."

Never give up—there's all sorts of wonderful things waiting for you just around the bend. I promise.